SPEAK EASY

© 2010 by Mary Lou Walker and Matthew Calkins

Published in Lafayette, California by Cupola Press®

Library of Congress Control Number: 2010927642

ISBN-13: 978-0-9793345-8-0
ISBN-10: 0-9793345-8-6

Printed in the United States of America

Speak easy

Mary Lou's Rules for Engaging Conversation

**Mary Lou Walker
& Matthew Calkins**

Cupola
PRESS®

www.cupolapress.com

CONTENTS

Introduction

"In my opinion, the most fruitful and natural play of the mind is in conversation. I find it sweeter than any other action in life; and if I were forced to choose, I think I would rather lose my sight than my hearing and voice."

MICHEL DE MONTAIGNE
(1533-1592) French essayist and humanist philosopher

At times it is difficult to have a good conversation; yet, at other times, the conversation flows from one topic to another, with wit and grace and occasional emotional or intellectual depth. What makes the difference?

The simple truth is that everybody talks, but few master the art of conversation. This book is an attempt to help spread the good word. My simple claim is this: If you practice the method of this book, you will become a better conversationalist. Whether you are already a sparkling asset to every party or painfully shy, observing the "rules" I have discovered for good conversation will improve your skills. If you then go on to join or form a conversational group or "colloquy," as I recommend, you will find a new and enduring source of joy in life, something you can use in all walks, and friends with whom you can talk of matters high, low, and in between.

Who am I to talk? Well, let's just say that I am a woman of a certain age. I've lived a full life, teaching, raising children, and traveling. I keep up with the world and stay busy with family, work, and friends. But two years ago I found myself increasingly frustrated and bored during conversations with my friends. It seemed as if all we could talk about were doctor visits and grandchildren. When, at long last, the talk turned to politics or other controversial subjects, it often became a polarized opinion stating session. Yet here we were, intelligent, informed people; surely we could do better than this.

Perhaps you can relate, no matter your age. If you are a parent, all you and your friends seem to talk about is your children. If you are single, the conversation may get stuck on school or work. Young children often feel captured at the dining table, not being schooled in the art of conversation—and their parents haven't learned to ask the kind of questions that elicit interest and answers beyond the monosyllabic.

What makes for a truly engaging conversation, appropriate to whatever group or subject is at hand? I, for one, wanted to find out and so embarked on a bit of research. In Part One of this book, I share some of the rules of the road (Mary Lou's Rules) that I learned along the way and began teaching in my Colloquy Class to help others become graceful and witty conversationalists.

Progress in all arts requires practice. One doesn't converse in a closet. Besides, the point is to be social in a new and fun way. And so in the second half of this book I describe various ways to get a group of people together for stimulating, witty, and informed conversation. Different sections are directed toward parents, library program directors, teachers, and people in business. By the end of the book—and with a bit of guided practice—no doubt you will find yourself taking a new role at dinner parties and family affairs, as the one who contributes a sparkling bon mot, offers a gracious invitation to a shy person, and receives the warm appreciation of all.

PART ONE

Mary Lou's Rules

1. Don't Steal the Subject

2. Rely on Raillery (Wit)

3. Avoid "I" Statements

4. Probe, Don't Pry

5. Participate, Don't Pontificate

6. Discuss, Don't Debate

7. Listen

8. Learn

9. Think Before You Speak

10. Keep Your Cool

Why Rules?

"If you don't like their rules, whose would you use?"

CHARLIE BROWN
Philosopher and cartoon character created by Charles Schulz

Rules are made to be broken, as the saying goes. But of course this implies that they must be learned, practiced, and understood before they can be broken to good effect. Rules are general guidelines that help us learn, keep us attentive, and remind us of pitfalls. In particular cases we must use our seasoned judgment.

With this caveat in mind, let us turn to Mary Lou's Rules for engaging conversation. They are not ranked in order of importance, but as a teaching series. The last rule ("Keep Your Cool") and next to last ("Think Before You Speak") are perhaps the most general and crucial—and most often unobserved! But, if you work your way through the ones listed before them, you may well find that they have already been achieved. In any case, bear with me. If a particular rule, such as avoiding "I" statements, is difficult to follow, don't just give up and move on; stick with it. Pay attention to how people actually talk. You will be surprised by your heightened awareness of what happens in most conversations. Though you may have difficulty observing the rule, at least you will become more observant.

This raises the larger point of why becoming adept in the art of conversation matters. Conversation matters because it is a large part of the art of living well, of becoming truly civilized. I am not talking about the search for self-fulfillment—enough of all that already. Nor do I wish to promote more self-aggrandizement. If you want to become a better public speaker and amaze the world with your awesome intellect and rhetorical splendor, this is not the book for you.

I am speaking of a way to help build community and become a better person. After all, the point of living is not mere existence, but fullness of life, and that includes much more than self-fulfillment. A full life includes the world around us keenly observed and cared for, other people respected and loved, a sense of the sheer mystery of existence, and our human calling to walk courageously into an unknown future. In this spirit, each chapter includes a reflection on a larger "life lesson" that pertains to the rule being presented. Chapters also include a brief sample dialogue, taken from one of my colloquy teaching classes, to further clarify an aspect of conversation.

Don't Steal the Subject

"The true spirit of conversation consists in building on another man's observation, not overturning it."

EDWARD G. BULWER-LYTTON
(1803-1873) British politician, poet and critic

How often has this happened to you? You are in a party conversation, telling the story of your trip somewhere—say, camping along the Colorado River. Someone jumps in and says that he and his family camped there once too, and then he proceeds to steal the subject and tell the story of his vacation. Sometimes this is even done with a sense of implied superiority: "Oh, yes, I know that campground—but did you get a chance to explore the canyon downstream? If you had been there for another day, as we were, you might have had the opportunity." Of course, you are internally seething, thinking—I wish your raft had overturned and you had a good soaking on that extra day!

Later we will talk about how to counter this kind of theft and smug one-upmanship with wit and raillery, but for now just think how frequently this happens. And admit that you do it, too! We all do. When we hear a story that triggers an association in our lives—whether people or places—we long to share it. Often we stop listening and politely wait for our turn—which may never come! Sometimes we rudely interrupt the current story and steal the subject. Of course, this is wrong—but so hard to resist. It happens with equal, or perhaps greater frequency, in political or other topical conversations. One idea or opinion or piece of news and gossip triggers thoughts of another, each person elbows in, and off it goes.

What to do? Go back to the previous paragraph. Note the observation that when an association is triggered we often stop paying full attention to the person talking and begin waiting for our turn to speak. There is a huge difference between listening and waiting to speak. Try and stay with listening and set the corollary incident aside for later (if it gets lost, it is not that important). Then, instead of stealing the subject, dig deeper. Ask questions. What was the funniest thing that happened on the trip? Was there a moment of beauty so awesome that you were moved outside of your self? Has this experience changed you? Provocative questions make for good conversation. People will be flattered by the attention but, even better, the conversation may take an interesting turn. It might move beyond recounting incidents and opinions to reflection or laughter (both of which are good).

President Barack Obama once said something that struck me in this regard when he was a student at Columbia University. The young Mr. Obama, showing something of the grace that would characterize his work as a community organizer and politician, said, "Everyone appreciates a kind word and a thoughtful response."

How true. Everyone appreciates being listened to and not interrupted. And no one, it is fair to say, is fond of having their story hijacked. Learn some manners. Wait your turn. Don't steal the subject.

LIFE LESSON: Civilizing Children

"Speech is civilization."

THOMAS MANN
(1875-1955) German author and critic

Dr. Perri Klass, pediatrician, journalist, author, and literacy advocate (and all around amazing woman), recently wrote an article in *The New York Times* about reforming rude children ("Making Room for Miss Manners Is a Parenting Basic," January 13, 2009). She writes that the essential job of parenting "is to start with a being who has no thought for the feelings of others, no code of behavior beyond its own needs and comforts—and, guided by love and duty, to do your best to transform that being into what your grandmother might call a *mensch*. To use a term that has fallen out of favor, your assignment is to 'civilize' the object of your affections."

As Judith Martin (Miss Manners) puts it, "Every child is born adorable but selfish and at the center of the universe. It's a parent's job to teach that there are other people and other people have feelings."

Learning to consider other people's feelings is the basis for moral development. Really, that's all that good manners are: speaking and acting with thoughtful consideration of other's feelings. Learning good manners is a big part of becoming a successful human being in the ways that really count.

Of course, there will always be some souls not cut out for the "civilized" world—and they will be right to leave it and even condemn it, if by "civilized" we mean a world where great wrongs are condoned in the name of law and order. On the first page of Mark Twain's *The Adventures of Huckleberry Finn,* thirteen-year-old Huck begins his story by remembering, "The Widow Douglas she took me for her son, and allowed she would sivilize [sic] me; but it was rough living in the house all the time, considering how dismal regular and decent the widow was in all her ways; and so when I couldn't stand it no longer I lit out."

Huck echoes this sentiment in the last line of the book, after the slave Jim has been freed, Tom Sawyer is recovering from being shot, and good Aunt Sally has offered to adopt the fourteen-year-old Huck. "But I reckon I got to light out for the territory ahead of the rest, because Aunt Sally she's going to adopt me and sivilize me, and I can't stand it. I been there before."

Huck would never become "sivilized," but he had already become a mensch. He passed the test when he made the decision to lie to the slave-catchers and be damned (so he'd been taught), rather than let Jim be caught and returned to slavery. If civilization is living with respect toward others, Huck was truly civilized.

DIALOGUE: Don't Steal My Vacation

Mary Lou: Speaking of travel, Joan, tell us about your recent trip to Italy.

Joan: It was marvelous. We toured Rome and Venice, of course—and they are full of sites and shops and things to do—but we loved our week in Tuscany most of all. We stayed at a lovely palazzo in the countryside, surrounded by cypress trees and fields, rented a car, and spent each day exploring a different small city. Well, I guess Florence counts as rather more than that—and to be in the presence of the genius of Michelangelo and the others was breathtaking. But if I had to rate my favorite it was Sienna and the little museum housing dozens of lovely Madonnas of the early Renaissance.

Albert: Were you there for the famous annual horse race in the city square?

Joan: No, we just missed that. They were setting up for it. All the banners for the various families and clans were out and there was definitely excitement in the air.

Albert: We had a chance to be there once, years ago. It was quite a spectacle.

Richard: Yes, well, Italy is all very nice, if you like crowds, churches and ruins. But give me the great outdoors anytime. We went last year on a boat ride up the Amazon—deep into the rainforest, visiting villages that seemed to suddenly appear out of the green and dense jungle, like tropical birds.

Paul: Italy, Brazil. Sounds like the World Cup. Which by the way happens to be coming up soon. Anyone here a soccer fan?

Alice: I used to play quite a bit—and you mean "football," don't you? That's what the rest of the world calls it.

Mary Lou: Our conversation seems to be wandering far afield. Could we get back to talking about travel? Joan and Richard sounded like they had wonderful trips—but I wonder what any of you would call the worst trip of your life? Jump right in, but don't drink the water.

Note in this discussion on travel that Joan has a chance to speak about her trip to Italy and her favorite places. Albert continued the discussion by asking a question and adding his own comment. Richard somewhat abruptly moved the group to South America, but I don't think this counts as a terrible example of stealing the subject. After all, the subject is travel. But clearly Paul's comment about soccer does completely change the subject—and Alice goes right along. Therefore, as facilitator, I jumped in to bring the discussion back to travel. One thing I could have done is ask someone who hadn't yet contributed to speak about her or his travels, but instead I tried to liven up the discussion by moving from the comparison of beautiful or exotic places to a potentially funny and interesting area: bad trips (we've all been on at least one).

2

Rely on Raillery (Wit)

"Repartee… is the highest order of wit, as it indicates the coolest yet quickest exercise of genius, at a moment when the passions are roused."

CHARLES CALEB COLTON
(1780-1832) British clergyman and author

Wit, my dears, will do more for a good conversation than eloquence. Golden words may be falling from the lips of one speaker, but is he or she dominating the conversation? Sometimes it is entertaining or instructive to sit at the feet of a great teacher or storyteller, but this is not conversation; it is performance, a different art. The key factors of a conversation are multiple person participation and a good-natured tone. This is where the art comes in. A good conversationalist knows how to inject a lighter tone to the discussion with wit to move away from a bore or an argument.

By wit, I mean good-natured teasing (raillery) and clever and apt turns of phrase. I do not mean cutting sarcasm and cruel humor, marks of immaturity and egotism. It may be amusing to witness a cutting competition—whether the outrageous insults of boys or the withering put-downs of girls—but this is watching a sport, sometimes a cruel sport, not participating in a conversation. Wit should be used as a tool, not a weapon; as a scalpel, not an axe or a blowtorch.

With wit comes the release of taking yourself too seriously, for the flip side of teasing is that you must be able to accept raillery with grace when it is aimed at you. By laughing along with everyone else, you defuse the threat that banter may get out of hand and become insult. This is not to say we should be bland and excessively fearful of giving offense; wit is the spice of conversation. But what one person considers a zinger may be taken as an insult by another. This is why conversation is an art, not a science. A good heart and openness to apologizing make the difference between insult and teasing. Rules—like manners—are guides that spell out a universal truth: don't do to others what you don't wish done to yourself.

Wit is most effective when conversation becomes heated or one-sided. When conversants become combatants, a light touch of wit calms ruffled feathers. When one person is holding forth, a deft jab moves her or him off balance and allows another voice to step in. In one of our colloquies, immigration became the topic, and the conversation quickly heated up. One person was indignant about "those people" taking American jobs, using taxpayer-supported services, and demanding another language besides English be accepted in official business. Another stepped up and counter punched with an opposing argument. After an exchange or two, it was clear that nobody was of a mind to change positions and continuing the discussion would generate lots of heat but no more light. A third voice stepped in and said, "I would like to *emigrate* to another topic. We have been talking about the flow of people across borders. What do you think about the way the world's economy is increasingly interconnected? Is that a good or a dangerous thing?" And with that light touch, we moved on.

LIFE LESSON: Humor and Marriage

"A happy marriage is a long conversation which always seems too short."

ANDRE MAUROIS
(1885-1967) French author and man of letters

Wit is wonderful within a conversation of friends, but good humor lightens the tone and lessens the destructive potential of conflict within a marriage or other intimate relationship as well. You do know, I suppose, that even great lovers have quarrels. Lousy lovers have them, too. A good marriage is not marked by the absence of conflict, but by how the spouses fight. John Gottman, a well-respected researcher and expert in marriage therapy, writes in his classic study *What Makes Marriages Work?*, "Fighting—when it airs grievances and complaints—can be one of the healthiest things a couple can do for their relationship (indeed, how you fight is one of the most telling ways to diagnose the health of your marriage)."

The good news is that any style, "validating, volatile or avoidant," can work. But whatever the style of conflict, the magic ratio of things said to and about each other should be roughly five positive to one negative. Heated exchanges need to be balanced by affection and humor. When the ratio is close to even, there's trouble in the relationship, and when there's more negative than positive, call the lawyers, it's as good as over! The walls go up and communication is no longer conversation but mortar fire returned with machine gun bursts. Humor used as a weapon isn't funny, but fatal. Add sarcastic insult to wounded feelings and you speed up the death spiral.

I've had my share of learning this lesson the hard way. But I'd rather not do it again, thank you very much. And there is a better way—learning from our mistakes, listening to good teachers, like Dr. Gottman. He writes that one of the key "repair mechanisms" for damaged relationships is humor. Of course, "no one can teach you how to be funny, but if you let yourself go, you may find yourself tickled by life's absurdities as well as your own. Humor starts with being able to laugh at yourself. It is a masterful way of handling a tense situation."

Life is funny, after all.

DIALOGUE: Politics and Wit

Mary Lou: We've been talking politics. I can hardly see through all the cigar smoke. John, you look as if you're about ready to explode. What is on your mind?

John: I've been listening to you all opinionate on world affairs and what you would do better—and one thing I know is I don't know. I am not as educated as you all are. I used to repair utility lines—a fairly cut and dry job. But even that isn't as easy to do as outsiders think. Now that I'm retired and have a chance to pick up books and take courses like this, well, it's wonderful to have opinions on everything, but how much do we really know about what it takes to pass health care reform or end a war in the Middle East?

Mark: Still, when it comes down to it, we all have to make a choice: do something or nothing. A vote is a decision after all, this or that, yes or no.

Alice: Maybe.

In this conversation I exercised my role as facilitator to give John a chance to speak. I could see he wanted to join in but the pace of opinion-stating was fast and getting furious. So I intervened with a bit of wit and deliberately gave John the floor. He made a good point. Mark then abruptly challenged the idea that we could remain on the sidelines and leave it up to the experts. Alice, who has a wonderful dry wit, moved quickly to defuse the confrontation with one well-placed word: "Maybe."

3

Avoid "I" Statements

"I often quote myself. It adds spice to my conversation."

GEORGE BERNARD SHAW
(1856-1950) Irish playwright, social critic, and wit

This is my favorite rule to teach because, if you learn to follow this rule, I guarantee a great change in the manner of your conversation. But it is also the hardest rule to follow. Many beginning students object to it because it counters one of our deepest-seated habits, putting "I" first.

Think about it. How often do you begin a sentence with the phrase "I think," or "I read in the paper," or "I heard on the radio," or "in my opinion"? But is it really necessary to preface the content part of your sentence with the obvious qualifier that it is your thought, opinion, or perception? Of course not. Who else's thought would it be? If you are repeating someone's else's comment, go straight to giving credit: "In the New York Times today," "Rush Limbaugh said the most outrageous thing," or, "As that great thinker, my mother, once said." If it is your thought or opinion, then simply state it. Your listeners know it is yours.

What difference does it make when we omit the prefatory "I"? For one thing, it avoids distraction and concentrates on

Remember, conversations are not a form of performance art.

the main point. "I" usage is a sort of conversational virus; it gets caught by others and spreads. If you think such and such, well, I think so and so. Notice how the point has become the difference between you and me, not the contrast in content. "I" statements introduce a subtle competition: who has thought, heard or read the most or the latest. As soon as you begin saying "in my humble opinion," others begin to think about how to deflate you—as they should. But if you simply begin with the thought or piece of information that is your main subject, attention will be focused on that, not you.

We see this turn to the "I" in another way as well, in the form of competitive anecdotes about one's own children, grandchildren, experiences, successes, and sufferings. This is really a form of stealing the subject, but it is also a way of letting the "I" overly determine the content of the conversation, to the detriment of its quality. Who enjoys listening to someone else wax on about his or her gifted grandchildren? Mine, of course, are absolutely priceless and practically perfect in every way (as Mary Poppins used to say), but I am sure you don't want to hear too much about them—or about my hip surgery, hearing aids, or driving accidents.

Unless, that is, I can package the tale of woe or triumph in an amusing story—and then it is the story that amuses; the "I" has become a character among others. This is wonderful, but difficult to do well, and poses a danger to the flow of conversation. Remember the point in rule number one that conversations are not a form of performance art? What is best in a conversation, as distinct from catching up with friends, or entertaining at a party, is *the focus on a subject, and the participation of many voices* in viewing that subject from various angles.

Finally, a great benefit of avoiding "I" statements is that by doing so you are forced to think before you speak. We all have the habit of using "I" unnecessarily. To get into the new habit of avoiding its use takes practice and requires a conscious screening before speaking. Silently editing what you are about to say helps you focus on the main point you are trying to get across. The clarity of your thought is heightened and the distracting "I" is set aside. Try it. It does take practice, but the work is worth it. You will find your comments become more pointed and the extra moment of thought encourages a bit of polish as well. You may even find a gift for epigrammatic wit waiting beneath the surface of a habitual pattern of "I"s (not to mention "likes"—the bane of the younger set). Subject a lump of coal to sufficient pressure and a diamond is formed. A bit of cutting and polish and, voila!, a sparkling gem.

LIFE LESSON: A Disclaimer

What is life for, if not for becoming someone people want to hear from? By that, I mean a real person, a man (or woman) in full, to borrow a phrase from the novelist Tom Wolfe. A person with virtues and flaws, not a paragon. Someone with character and experience, as well as knowledge and wit. You may not (yet) be the person you can be. You may not, in your own self-estimation, be someone worth listening to. Or you may have the opposite problem: you may not be God's gift to the world that you think you are. The truth is probably somewhere in between.

Each person has something to offer, a unique perspective at the very least. No other human being in the history or the future of the world occupies your exact place in space and time. None have your eyes to see what you see, and your mind alone is home to your thoughts, unless you choose to share them. Not every thought is worth sharing. Most aren't. But every self is. And that is where this rule—Avoid "I" Statements—needs to be broken. For it is in conversation that moves into deeper levels of trust and intimacy, where we share our truest and deepest selves, that "I" statements have their place.

Twelve-step programs, begun by the founders of Alcoholics Anonymous, have made great contributions to the amount of honest conversations in the world. They begin with the admission of a weakness—my name is Jane or Joe and I am an alcoholic or drug addict. This admission is always bought at the very high price of failure and shame, a bargain none of us would choose, but which is better than a life of continuing addiction. If Socrates was right that an unexamined life is not worth living, then at least all of this has led to increased self-knowledge. But I wouldn't suggest bringing into casual conversation the hard lessons and current problems of our lives; that would be "way too much information," as my grandchildren are fond of saying. But for those honest conversations about deep and hard subjects, when people are revealing core convictions and strong emotions, then the rule about not using "I" to begin sentences may need to be reversed.

As many professional mediators and marital therapists will tell you, it is best, in responding to a painful or emotional subject, to use "I" language. Reflect back what you have heard ("this is what I hear you saying…") so that the person you are talking with feels both listened to and understood, and then—even if you still disagree—couch your response in an "I" form: "But I feel," or "I think," or "I have come to believe." This approach steers the conversation away from being confrontational and can even make your disagreements seem agreeable.

DIALOGUE: Politics and Wit

Mary Lou: We've been working on avoiding excessive use of personal pronouns, and I am proud of you. Now don't point your finger, John. It is perfectly alright to use "I" when referring to one's own mental state or action as the main subject of the sentence. What we want to avoid are unnecessary prefaces to statements that can stand perfectly well on their own without being told that "I" believe them.

Alice: I agree.

John: Good one, Alice. But I still think this is a crazy rule. What am I supposed to say, just, this is a crazy rule?

Mary Lou: Yes. Then I can reply, no, it is a good rule. It is a good rule because it makes us think. Look at the way the world has gone overboard on celebrity culture. It is all about ego and fame and the rest of the world acting as audience.

Bill: What is it about celebrities that we find so fascinating? Why are there more entertainment news programs than world and national news programs?

Joan: Because the floods and wars on the news program are scary—our own lives could be overturned like that—and we wish they were more like red carpets and passionate affairs.

Alice: Passionate affairs overturn lives too—look at all these politicians going down in flames.

Mary Lou: Well, at least they give us plenty to talk about. It's a lot more entertaining than the over-use of the first-person singular.

Here is an example of a conversation that includes a bit of teaching about the way to approach the rule, "Avoid 'I' Statements." This rule always generates a great deal of discussion and opposition—though after a few weeks of practice, students appreciate the way this rule helps them get directly to the point. It's a good rule, don't you agree? Note that adding "don't you agree" or "wouldn't you say" to the end of a statement of opinion is an alternative to saying, "I think"—one that has an interesting way of inviting others into agreement rather than opposition and which encourages further discussion on the subject.

4

Probe, Don't Pry
(Agitate, Don't Irritate)

"There is no such thing as a worthless conversation, provided you know what to listen for. And questions are the breath of life for a conversation."

JAMES NATHAN MILLER
Journalist, author

This rule puts good manners in tension with provocative questioning. It is an important rule for negotiating the borderline between the causal conversation (which can be boring and trivial) and the provocative and substantial one (which can become threatening and invasive).

The basis for the rule is the difference between the personal and the private. Each of us has personal involvement and experience in various public and private spheres: family, church, community, school, work, politics, and so on. When we talk about subjects in the public sphere, as we do in a conversation about topics of interest in our world, we naturally bring our personal perspective to bear. It is quite alright, even unavoidable, to speak from one's personal point of view. (This, indeed, is why it is unnecessary and distracting to say that it is "I" who is thinking, speaking, etc.) But if we state a fact or make a claim, then we invite interrogation:

What we do not wish to be made public
should be kept private.
A conversation is not a confession.

"How do you know such and such?" What is the basis for your claim that so and so?" These are probing questions. And they will get personal, just as our answers will. "This is my experience and my opinion. I am entitled to claim it and defend it." If this exchange sounds a bit testy, try gentle probing inquiries such as: "Tell us about your involvement in civil rights." "What was it like growing up in China?" Either way, here's the point of the rule: in some cases you may decide that an inquiry touches upon a personal matter that is too private and not open to public conversation.

During a wide-ranging conversation, it is important to be aware of this border zone between the personal and the private, both for your own sake and for others'. There is no sharp demarcation. You have to decide what to withhold and how hard to push, if at all. This is why there is tension between good manners and necessary provocation. Our emotions and sense of self are intimately tied up with our concepts and stories. We are not speaking as disembodied strangers, aloof and invulnerable. We speak and share as neighbors, friends, members of a shared community. What we do not wish to be made public should be kept private. A conversation is not a confession. Although certainly we should respect the wishes of someone who would like what he or she says to remain confidential, this is not a general expectation of a topical conversation. These days, people are apt to share too much. Discretion is a virtue less practiced than it ought to be. It is simply good manners to respect another's privacy. Probe but don't pry.

"Agitate, Don't Irritate" is a variation of this rule. "Probe, Don't Pry" suggests we can get personal while still respecting privacy; "agitate, don't irritate" invites us to combat complacency without becoming overly aggressive and rude. This is not only a matter of probing for reasons and asking for evidence. To agitate means to stir things up, get things going, raise the temperature a bit during a flat conversation. Settled and stale opinions deserve to be dislodged. It is often the case that we are used to conversing with people who agree with us or who are too polite to disagree publicly. Without the willingness to be provocative, to ask probing questions, to agitate and stir things up, the conversation will lapse into platitudes and boredom.

Conversation is not a contest—we are not looking for winners and losers—but is an arena in which experience and opinions venture into the open to be met by the experiences and opinions of others. Our personal opinions are questioned on their merits. This is good. It tests our thoughts and experience. It makes for new insight and energy. Nothing new is said in an echo chamber.

LIFE LESSON: Politics and Sex

One of the things I love to do is to express an outrageous opinion just to get things moving (I have a bit of the devil in me). In political discussions, I often take the side the majority seems to have decided against. It's okay to be provocative, even occasionally outrageous, in the cause of good conversation.

Another way to get things going is to state a claim (it hardly matters what; someone will disagree) about the differences between men and women or the changes (for better or worse) in mating habits among generations. When a little old lady talks about sex, people listen, let me tell you. Remember Dr. Ruth? The younger folks sit up, and it is amusing to see embarrassment flash across their faces. Every generation thinks it was the first to find out about the facts of life.

Certainly it is much more acceptable to talk about sex than when I was young (nothing sex-related was said in the presence of a young lady then). But for a conversation, hints and wit work better than gross-out humor or explicit description. Watch a Mae West movie or any of the old screwball comedies and listen for the delicious double entendres. (Said the man to Mae West: "Madam, you are wrong; I will lay you ten to one." Mae in reply: "It's an odd time, but you're on.")

Politics and sex usually work to get the conversation

going, but to what end? Well, a good conversation is its own justification (just like a good meal). But we also converse as part of a greater project: being active in the world. In this sense, agitation is a means to get us to do something, to get us off our seats and stop just talking about it (whatever "it" is). Not every conversation will or ought to lead to action, but sometimes we talk as a step toward actually making a difference in the world. Here, indeed, is what community organizing is after, a recognition of the gap between the world as it is and the world as it ought to be.

Conversations that probe and explore this difference, which all of us must feel, lead us to a conviction that something should be done to close the gap. It's time to agitate. Here the conversation can fruitfully be turned to questions about our next steps. What are we personally going to do about this problem that we have so eloquently laid out? A washing machine has an agitation cycle; the purpose is to clean clothes. Sure, the world has problems we love to talk about. But what are we going to do about them? That's a question not asked often enough. That's the purpose of a probing conversation.

"He has the right to criticize if he has the heart to help."

ABRAHAM LINCOLN
(1809-1865) 16th President of the United States

DIALOGUE: Small Talk Dancing

Joan: Probe, don't pry; I wonder where to draw the line. How about those awkward moments when you've just met someone and you're trying to figure out if they are in a serious relationship or unattached?

Alice: It was easier when the options were married or single and you could look at someone's left hand ring finger for the answer.

Bill: I also notice that when people meet, there are a lot of initial questions about what business they are in—a kind of reconnaissance mission on each part.

Joan: True—and so boring, the small talk dance. How about we make it a rule to meet new people and not ask about work or family? Instead we can use our new conversational skills to say something provocative about current events or people in the news.

Alice: Where do you stand, Joan, on health care reform?

Joan: Good question. I suppose the next one is, "And what are you going to do about it?"

Alice: (laughing) No, I was going to open it to the group: What are we going to do about it?

In this small snippet of conversation, Joan asks the group a question that is something of a personal concern as well. Clearly, she has come to trust the people in the group not to make fun of her. Indeed, the conversation goes on to talk in a general way about how we send personal signals and assess others through small talk and details of dress. Joan then decides to move the conversation to a different plane—current events—and Alice does a bit of probing by following up with a direct question on her views regarding health care. Joan understands what she is doing-and the two of them move the abstract discussion to a practical level: what are we going to do about it.

5

Participate, Don't Pontificate

"Ideal conversation must be an exchange of thought, and not, as many of those who worry most about their shortcomings believe, an eloquent exhibition of wit or oratory."

EMILY POST
(1872-1960) Author on etiquette, advice columnist

Read widely, expand your understanding, share your insights, but don't pontificate. A bore casts a deadly pall on a conversation. What is a bore? One who insists on holding forth long past the moment, if there was one, when what he or she had to say was basically understood. Pedants and bores don't know when enough is enough. Perhaps the details of a transmission repair, the complexity of credit derivatives, or the manifold malfeasance of a politician are interesting to you, but to a larger group the interest passes once the general point is grasped. To go on at length does not add to our understanding, it simply loses our interest. It is far better to state the general idea, give a telling detail or thumbnail summary, and stop. If the incident, idea, or news item is gripping, others in the group will ask questions and probe for details. It is much more interesting for a group to watch two (or more) people go back and forth exploring

To go on at length does not add to our understanding—
it simply loses our interest.

a topic than it is to watch a lecture (unless, of course, the speaker is a gifted lecturer—an expert in the subject with a flair for explanation). But here, again, we have moved from conversation, the exchange of words, to a performance, however enlightening or gripping. Good conversationalists are measured by "the pleasure they give, not the information they impart" (David Hume, a Scottish philosopher and historian in the age of Enlightenment).

The opposite of a bore is a mouse. If some can't stop talking, others seem unable to start. This may be due to shyness or fear. Sometimes there is a sort of truculent unwillingness to engage in conversation (try getting polite dinner conversation out of a moody teenager). Sometimes the quiet person simply has not yet mastered the art of jumping in and joining the flow. Some people grow up in a talkative family where hardly a sentence is allowed to reach its period; others are raised in a more quiet and taciturn household. It may be hard for the latter to get a word in edgewise with the former. Here it is the responsibility of the facilitator of the conversation—a person acknowledged as such or simply willing and able to perform the function—to stop the flow and invite the reluctant sideliner to step in.

It is not only polite but a matter of fairness for all to participate. If I may offer another quotation from a master of the art: "To keep quiet when others are engaged in conversation seems to show an unwillingness to pay one's share of the bill" (Giovanni Della Casa, an arbiter of society mores in the Italian Renaissance). Everyone has a personal perspective, just as everyone has a body. It is often helpful in a conversation to have someone speak from a position of ignorance and ask basic questions; sometimes common sense questions lay bare unfounded assumptions. If you are shy, steel yourself, and simply offer a question or something you have heard. If you are feeling superior, go on, offer your expert opinion—short and to the point—and see if the crowd buys it. To remain on the sidelines while all others are speaking poses an unspoken question: are you shy or superior? Jump in, the water is fine. Nothing makes skinny-dipping less fun than having some of the party remain on shore fully clothed. (I may be a grandmother, but I'm not a prude; and, although it is hard to believe now, I once was shy as a mouse.)

LIFE LESSON: LESS is More

In conversation LESS is more:

*L*isten

*E*mpathize

*S*elf-monitor

*S*peak

I will go into more detail on how to actively **Listen** in rule number seven. There is an art to it and without engaged listeners there is not a conversation, just a series of soapbox speeches.

To **Emphathize** with others is to realize that we all have more in common than we know. It doesn't mean we all agree. It means we can share understandings and feelings. *Pathos* is the root of the word: feeling, emotion. Sym-pathy means feeling *with* another. Em-pathy, a very similar word, means feeling or understanding *into* another. The point of empathy is understanding, not agreement. I can empathize without sympathy; that is, I can understand your thoughts and feelings without necessarily agreeing with or approving of them. I might have sympathy for your job loss, but not for your anger at getting fired (I might think you deserved it). But, through empathy, I understand both. And notice that empathy is also subtly different than simply stating, "I understand what you're saying." To empathize is to grasp the *feeling* as well as the idea. We often get the meaning of a sentence without grasping what the subject "means" to the person. Sometimes this is an exercise of imagination. A young person must try to imagine what it feels like to be the older person who is speaking—what it is like to have a lot more of life in the rear view mirror than on the road ahead.

Sometimes it is a work of memory that helps us empathize. Indeed, memory and imagination are the twin keys to empathy. Bear in mind (remember, imagine) what it is like to be the person speaking. Life is full of wonder and terror, hope and disappointment. These are powerful emotions for all ages. When you sense them beneath the words about school and work, doctors and deliveries, even if quite muted, you should be thrilled: you are empathizing.

To **Self-monitor** is to watch yourself from the balcony seats. How often are you speaking, how emotional are you getting, or how distanced and quiet are you appearing? Of course we mostly want to stay on the dance floor, especially with such wonderful conversational partners. But every once in a while, take a quick hike to a higher view. It helps to have a role in the group as someone who helps facilitate as well as participate. Even if this is not your "official" position you can notice the participation of others. Clara is very quiet; is something wrong? Maybe she has hurt feelings, or maybe she is just shy. Perhaps she is simply listening. Old curmudgeon Harry is having trouble with respect for the opinions of others. He might need an elbow, so to speak, a touch of barbed raillery. And now look at yourself. Have you been involved too much or too little? Self-monitoring will help you control your tongue (more on this in the rule "Think Before You Speak"). Yes, this involves practice and discipline. But I never said mastering the art of conversation was going to be easy.

DIALOGUE: Human Interest

John: And here's another reason why the Obama health plan is such a disaster.

Lauren: John, I have sat here listening to you rattle on about Congress, the President and health care for ten minutes. Don't you remember the rule, "Participate Don't Pontificate?"

John: Well, go on then. What do you think should be done?

Lauren: Something rather than nothing. Because what we have now is not working—and that is plain to everyone. But I'm frankly less interested in policy discussions than hearing from the rest of you on how your lives have been affected by the health care system.

Short but not so sweet: Lauren cuts John off a bit harshly here, but then he has been rattling on. What impresses me in this example though is how Lauren doesn't just take the stage for her turn, but opens it up to the rest of the group—and invites them to share personal stories rather than discuss dry policies. Personal stories are engaging and memorable, and that is why good journalists almost always start their articles with a human interest angle. Try using this technique in conversation, too.

Discuss, Don't Debate

"A man accustomed to hearing only the echo of his own sentiments, soon bars all the common avenues of delight, and has no part in the general gratification of mankind."

DR. SAMUEL JOHNSON
(1709-1784) The dean of English conversationalists

This rule is similar to number five, "Participate, Don't Pontificate." Both rules help guide us away from potential problems in a group conversation. Rule five seeks to avoid the problem of an individual dominating the conversation; the aim of rule six is to avoid the problem of two or more people turning a discussion into debate. What happens then is that the tone of the conversation becomes charged with emotion, and conversational partners become partisan opponents. But a colloquy—the sort of interesting and enlivening conversation this book hopes to cultivate—is a lighter, yet more difficult, sort of conversation. It requires wit, courtesy, and a genuine desire to hear out and understand the ideas and experiences of others. We converse to enjoy each other's presence and point of view, not to score points or change minds. "We must learn the art of conversation, from which truth emerges not, as in Socratic dialogues, by the refutation of falsehood, but from the quite different process of letting our world be enlarged by the presence of others who think, act, and interpret reality in ways radically different from our own" (Jonathan Sacks).

Of course, when we discuss such topics as politics or religion, it can be very hard to avoid ruffling feathers. Strongly worded opinions will offer sharp contrasts. Emotional investment in one's perspective will release a surge of adrenaline and it may be hard to restrain angry or biting responses. This does not mean that some subjects, say abortion or war, are off the table, but the facilitator must be very mindful of the need to regulate the temperature of the conversation and to introduce notes of grace and humor.

Compare politics and sports. Both have their partisans, or, as they say of sports, fans. Both have contests with winners and losers, involve pre-contest prognostication, and post-game or election-result analysis. But a good sports discussion between knowledgeable fans of opposing teams—where I live, we have Yankees and Red Sox fans in close proximity—generally maintains a sense of perspective. It is understood that players on both sides are excellent athletes trying as hard as they can, and in the end the game is only a game. Naturally, there is good-natured ribbing and boasting. But friends remain friends, however misplaced their team loyalties. "It's great that the Red Sox finally won a World Series or two; now the long wait can begin again." "Do you mean the drought of championships that began when A-Rod signed?" And so on. Granted, given enough alcohol and testosterone (or envy and estrogen, to be fair to the female fanatics among us), any conversation can become combative, but it's far better (and more fun) to maintain a sense of perspective.

Life is not a game, though play is an important part of life, and not taking ourselves too seriously is something akin to the virtue of humility. Politics and religion can and do involve matters of life and death. People have deep convictions about the meaning and purpose of life and often have strong biases against those of other faiths or no faith, this party or that country. Here the facilitator of a conversation must be alert. The point of the conversation is to encourage the sharing of information, opinions, and experience. By sharing, we learn the basis of political leanings, the experience that leads to different world views. The wonderful and overarching aim of the art of conversation is to encourage a civil society in which politics can be discussed without fear or hatred, religious difference with respect and interest. All around the world and throughout history, we see religion can become a weapon of division and war, in sharp contrast to the actual teaching of most religions on the values of compassion, justice, and peace. Rabbi Jonathan Sacks, whom I quoted above, is the chief rabbi of London. The title of the book from which I quoted, *The Dignity of Difference,* sums up the two key parts of a well-ordered society in this age of globalization and interconnection: dignity and difference. If we can begin with a core agreement on the dignity of every human being, and so treat each other with respect, then we can also appreciate the amazing diversity of our cultures and perspectives, and the richness this brings to our world.

LIFE LESSON: Going Deep

Ronald Rolheiser, a monk from Canada—isn't it wonderful to have rabbis and monks available for our conversation?—has written a number of books on culture and spirituality. In one of them, *The Holy Longing,* he makes the case that our very life force (call it libido, chi, or, as he does spirit) comes out shaped by our "holy longing" for meaning and purpose. Sometimes that leads to faith in God, sometimes not, but we all have a kind of spirituality that is our human way of expressing our deepest longings.

Brother Rolheiser uses three very different women to illustrate his point: Janis Joplin, Princess Diana, and Mother Teresa. Quite a group. But think about it: all of them had a tremendous amount of life energy; they were charismatic, compelling, talented people. But they differed greatly in how they directed their energy, their longing. 1960s rock star Joplin wanted it all and wanted it now. She lived life with burning intensity, trying to experience everything and do everything. She died very young. It is hard to imagine she could have lived long that way in any case. Princess Di also died young after a very bright and brief moment on the world stage. In her position as the center of the world's attention, she seemed both comfortable with the camera and drawn to work in charity; she enjoyed the dizzy social calendar of the wealthy and aristocratic, as well as helping the unfortunate of the world. Her energy and identity were not as diffuse and unsustainable as Joplin's, but split in two and somewhat at odds. Mother Teresa is, of course, the model of single focus. Her indomitable will to help the poor was what made her a wonder of the world, and a gift from God to the dying poor on the streets of Calcutta.

So what does this have to do with our discussion? Imagine for a moment a conversation with these three women, what they might share, how they might differ. I imagine their conversation going into some interesting places. I imagine them discussing, not debating. Imagine, too, if you were there in their midst. What would you add? You don't have to be famous to be fascinating. Share who you are. A full life will play itself out differently for each of us. Being respectful, genuinely interested, and willing to be open and share yourself is one way to get in touch with your own "holy longing" and notice the deep longings in others.

DIALOGUE: Don't Take The Bait

Mary Lou: Discuss, don't debate. Sounds good, but how do we draw the line?

Alice: I begin to debate when, instead of simply presenting my opinion, I try to change yours.

John: But what if I object to something you've said? Don't I have the conversational right to offer a counterpoint?

Alice: If you disagree with me and then present your own view, you are not necessarily trying to change my view.

John: Maybe not, but I am trying to convince others that I am right. Isn't that a sort of debate?

Alice: I refuse to take the bait.

Mary Lou: And so we see, wit is a wonderful way out.

This is a nice exchange between Alice and John that illustrates the rule while discussing it (or is it a debate?). Of course, the point is not to draw a hard and fast distinction but to keep a thought and tone in mind. Civility is the key, as well as respect for the opinions and feelings of others. And of course I love it when people use a bit of wit (even with a pun).

7

Listen

"Listening is a magnetic and strange thing, a creative force. The friends who listen to us are the ones we move toward, and we want to sit in their radius. When we are listened to, it creates us, makes us unfold and expand."

KARL MENNINGER
(1893-1990) Psychiatrist and author

"To listen closely and reply well is the highest perfection we are able to attain in the art of conversation."

FRANCOIS DE LA ROCHEFOUCAULD
(1613 - 1680) French author and moralist

Permit me to return to a few sentences from rule one: "Don't Steal the Subject": There is a huge difference between listening and waiting to speak. Try and stay with the listening, setting the corollary incident aside for later (if it gets lost, it is not that important). Then, instead of stealing the subject, interrogate it. Ask questions.

Listening is an art in itself. Indeed, a whole discipline of psychoanalysis has grown up around careful analytic listening. Normally, we do not converse to analyze the motives and character of others (though these are revealed in everything we do). But it is amazing how much can be learned from close attention to what is being said, what is not being said, and the language of the body, both that of the speaker and the listeners. A term such as "active listening" helps us get at what is wanted. An active listener is an engaged listener, with focused attention and body language that signals interest. You may agree or disagree with what is being said, but you are not bored, distracted or fidgety, waiting for your turn to speak.

After all, what do you want when it is your turn? You want engaged, attentive listeners for yourself. What happens when you have cut someone off? Hackles go up, eyes blaze, a belligerent or withdrawn posture is struck. If someone is droning on, attention wanders, bodies stretch, mouths yawn, and eyes flicker around the room. But if speaker succeeds speaker in pithy sequence, keeping to the subject or turning it in interesting ways, if laughter or a well-posed question varies the mood and pace, then we find all engaged, eager, and actively listening. It is true, others are waiting their turn to speak; but, well trained in the art of conversation, they are patient and continue to return to the speaker until the point is made.

Remember, listening is fifty percent of conversation. It is not a nuisance to be ignored or endured impatiently. It is important and ought to be done well. Pay attention to your posture and those around you. Do not underestimate the messages silently being communicated. If you do not learn to listen well, you will never master the art of speaking well in conversation.

LIFE LESSON: Good for Business

Whether you work in teaching, as I have most of my life, or business, public service, or charitable and religious work, listening well is an art you need for success. From Dale Carnegie a few generations ago to Stephen Covey and others today, this is the simple truth that sales and management gurus teach. The key to increasing sales and influencing people is not a gift for persuasive rhetoric, but rather a talent for understanding people. And how can you understand someone unless you listen to her or him?

You may reply, this is obvious. You can point to the prevalence of focus groups and consumer surveys as evidence that listening to the customer is common practice these days. Even the computers are listening. If you order books through Amazon or rent movies online, pretty soon you start receiving suggestions for books and movies based on your buying patterns. There is a huge industry devoted to researching consumer desires and finding magic formulas for subtly motivating the reluctant buyer. Forget love potions; the real action is in ad incantations.

But on what level are you really listening, and to what needs or wants are you responding? We all know that some people try to fool customers into buying something they don't need or truly want, something shoddy but glossy, not quite right, but what the boss wants moved. This is superficial listening and short-term thinking. As my friend, Skip Morse, writes about in the last chapter of this book, if you treat your clients and customers with true respect and really listen to them, they will respond with increased attention to what you have to say and offer. Asking for feedback and responding with appropriate changes are key to creating a long-term relationship. As Skip puts it regarding an advertising agency, "I'm tired of an agency pitching ideas. I want a business partner, not just a vendor. I want somebody who understands my industry, my challenges, my goals—and then comes back to give me solid advice about moving ahead."

It works in management as well as sales. Carol Bartz, the chief executive officer of Yahoo, was interviewed recently about the art of managing (*New York Times,* October 18, 2009). Asked how she hired people, Bartz answered that it is more than finding people who know their business (if they are qualified enough to get to her, she assumes that much). "I'm looking for a personality fit. I use humor in my management." She takes the prospective hire to dinner and *has a conversation.* If a person is too boring or buttoned up—red flag. Bartz is good at asking questions; she expects her top people to be good at giving answers—and asking good questions in return. Commenting on annual reviews, she answered, "The annual review process is so antiquated. I almost would rather ask each employee to tell us if they've had a meaningful conversation with their manager this quarter."

So you see, sales strategies and management review processes come and go, but the art of listening, a key part of the art of conversation, is perennial.

DIALOGUE: Stories are for Listening

Joan: Have you ever watched congressional hearings? The senators or congressmen are more interested in making speeches than getting answers. And talk about body language! The whole arrangement is designed to make one side look powerful and the other side squirm.

Peter: The people on the hot seat, whether cabinet officials or business people or military, agonize over their answers.

Joan: But the only thing that will be reported or remembered will be the gaffes.

John: That's why they agonize.

Peter: True—many times. But I've watched when ordinary people are invited to tell their story— usually a heartbreaking one or a story about overcoming obstacles—and they can be very moving.

Stories are easier to listen to than speeches. If you must give a speech, keep it short, or try to work a story or two into it. In this example, Joan and Peter share observations on the sort of soapbox congressional hearings that hardly resemble true conversations. With all that oratory, the real-life personal stories catch our attention and keep us listening.

A good conversationalist is marked by a variety of interests
and a decent range of knowledge.

Learn

"Human understanding is marvelously enlightened by daily conversation with men, for we are, otherwise, compressed and heaped up in ourselves, and have our sight limited to the length of our own noses."

MICHEL DE MONTAIGNE
(1533-1592) French essayist and courtier

If you are reading this, I will wager that you have spent many hours attending classes in your youth, and—here you are—an adult learner. Your shelves are well-stocked with books. You have traveled, here or abroad, more or less. If you cannot quote great poems, or rattle off the theories of philosophy and science, still you have heard of them. The history of kings and queens, wars and religion, our country and the world, and the mysteries of the cosmos may not all be clearly labeled and ordered in your mental file cabinet, but they are in there somewhere, somewhat accessible.

If your mind is like mine, it's like a closet stuffed full, mixed up, and tumbling out, with a perfect recall of television theme songs where great literature ought to be. Perhaps you prefer the movie to the book, but at least you are not entirely captive to television. Other interests may include walking in a gallery or along the shore, sports or volunteer work.

Whatever the variation, a good conversationalist is marked by a variety of interests and a decent range of knowledge. Furthermore, people of experience have a hard-won wisdom gained from loss as well as success and a perspective on the way the world works—or doesn't work—that's worth sharing.

Yet how often we find people attending classes, reading books, or returning from travel with little opportunity to talk and share! This indeed is what motivated me to begin this work. I have many well-educated and widely experienced friends, yet we seemed to be stuck in trivial conversations. Some try book clubs—and this is wonderful as far as it goes—but there the subject is captive, whereas conversation wants to be free. Sometimes, those who have attended my colloquy sessions complain that they can no longer endure the conversations of their friends. They are too stifled and small-minded. The answer is not (or not only) to make new friends, but also to spread your wider willingness to converse. Learners become teachers, and the good news spreads.

Learning should be lifelong—a platitude that rolls off our lips yet is not so easy to practice. I have found that engagement in a regular conversation group encourages continued learning. If you know that a certain subject will be discussed, then you will find yourself dusting off a relevant book and rereading it (or, as my grandchildren do, Googling it and consulting Wikipedia). Since current news and issues of the day will certainly be part of the conversation, you find yourself giving the paper more than a cursory glance and perhaps even reading longer articles in *The Economist* or other journals. Aware that the group has certain expectations concerning participation, you find yourself mentally rehearsing your thoughts and examining your opinions and those of others. The result is, you become more aware of the world and of what you yourself think about it. You have profited from the colloquy before even participating in it!

LIFE LESSON: Use it or Lose It

"I've often thought that the process of aging could be slowed down if it had to go through Congress."

GEORGE HERBERT BUSH
41st President of the United States

Growing old is not easy. Having entered my eighties, I can report with authority. Personally, I am greatly blessed—I am a survivor of melanoma cancer and various other indignities. I remain energetic, active, and reasonably coherent. But such has not been the case for many of my dear friends and loved ones. I have become far too familiar with funeral services. Equally difficult has been watching friends decline into dementia or Alzheimer's disease. Is there any help for these conditions in mental exercises, such as doing crossword puzzles or engaging in stimulating conversations?

I hope so.

Scientific research seems to support this hope, to a limited degree. The National Institute on Aging has been studying the issue for years. Their conclusion is that normal healthy aging is distinguished from diseases that can afflict the aged, such as diabetes or dementia. There is no single timetable for getting old; we all age differently, and a combination of genetics, lifestyle, and disease affect the rate of aging. You may be stuck with your genes, but lifestyle and exposure to disease is partly within your control. Exercise (physical and mental) and diet do make a difference. One researcher, Dr. David Snowdon, studying 678 nuns of ages 75 to 100 plus, has written a book, *Aging with Grace,* about a correlation between youthful "idea density" (as found in written spiritual autobiographies and other materials) and resistance to dementia.

Even if you misspent your youth—and who didn't; my generation drank and smoked too much, our children took drugs, and who knows what the grandchildren are up to—the brain doesn't stop growing new cells. According to an article in *Scientific American,* "Fresh neurons arise in the adult brain every day. New research suggests that the cells ultimately help with learning complex tasks—and the more they are challenged, the more they flourish" (Tracey Shorrs, "Saving New Brain Cells," March 2009).

But even if new brain cells are produced, they will disappear if the brain isn't "cognitively challenged." So do a crossword puzzle, learn a new language, take up bridge, and share your acquired knowledge with others by joining a challenging conversation group!

DIALOGUE: The Hard Way

Mary Lou: If we read about something in the paper or attend a lecture on a subject, we may learn something. But knowing is a deeper thing, isn't it?

Alice: Definitely. Or anyway, knowing about something is different than knowing something. I know a little about a lot of celebrities, but I don't know any of them.

John: Most of what I learned in school I have forgotten—who remembers the periodic table?—but what I have practiced and used outside of school, that's the sort of thing I know.

Joan: It's funny, but some of the things we know the best, like tying a shoelace or how to ride a bicycle, are really hard to explain to others. You just have to learn it for yourself.

Peter: Like the value of a dollar, or a true friend. When we are young we take a lot for granted; we assume things will always be the same.

John: Unless you lose a parent when you're young. Then the world seems a very dangerous place.

Peter: I'm sorry—did you lose a parent when you were a child?

John: Yes. Some lessons are learned the hard way.

Here we see how a straightforward conversation can enter into personal disclosure. Learning is not only a matter of mastering subjects and skills but finding out about other people. To get to the stage in which people are comfortable in sharing personal information, you will need to develop trust. Trust is fostered when what we've been discussing in this book has been practiced with some consistency. For example, when humor is good-willed and not cutting and when listeners are patient and not prying, people will sense that it is safe to share. Possibly what is most important for establishing a learning, trusting atmosphere is adherence to the final two rules: "Think Before You Speak" and "Keep Your Cool."

9

Think Before You Speak

"Do you see a man who speaks in haste? There is more hope for a fool than for him."

PROVERBS 29:20

Who would disagree with this rule? Who has not regretted saying something hurtful or stupid the second it has passed their lips? Many a politician has learned, to his or her dismay, how closely people listen when a gaffe is made— no matter how many hours of golden oration may precede or follow. On a more intimate scale, you know that an unkind comment or a joke turned slightly sour is remembered far more keenly than the speaker generally intends. (If you do intend to cut or ridicule someone, then perhaps a friendly colloquy is not the place for you.)

The proverbial nature of this rule (think before you speak, look before you leap) reflects the fact that it is common sense. And yet we all let a foolish or unkind word slip occasionally, even the wisest and most thoughtful of us. The thing to do then is to admit one's mistake, ignorance, or unkindness, and simply and clearly apologize.

It would be better, though, to practice careful speaking, which is the spouse of active listening.

Careful speaking is the spouse of active listening.
Many happy hours can be shared between the two.

You may be thinking, Mary Lou, this is all very well to say, but the give and take of conversation allows little time to measure one's words. True, there may be little time, but use what you have and mentally rehearse at least the following checklist.

Are you speaking in anger or with contempt?
Perhaps someone has already struck a match and started you smoldering inside. Then there is a good chance that your response could fan the fire. Our final rule below—Keep Your Cool—will do much to prevent responses that you will regret.

Are you speaking in jest?
Then check the quip or joke for slurs or mean spirit. Racial, ethnic, and group jokes (lawyers, blondes, etcetera) usually fall flat, if not outright offend. If you cannot help repeating a joke you have heard, use one that is directed at a group you are part of (lawyers telling lawyer jokes and so on). Be aware that you do not know the intimate history of those around you. Observe the golden rule.

Are you being careful with confidences?
People have trusted you with private stories and intimate feelings; be careful not to refer to them out of context or in the heat of conversation. Not only do you betray the trust of your friend, you harm your own reputation as someone who can be trusted.

Are you repeating gossip?
If you have heard through the grapevine a juicy piece of

gossip, keep it to yourself. Usually it is of dubious truth, and repeating it reflects poorly on you. Some restraint applies to gossip about celebrities and politicians, too, although repeating this stuff is almost irresistible. We laugh at and freely criticize the rich, famous, and powerful—and perhaps that is just desserts—but often it is just sour grapes. Check yourself for a spirit of envy or bitterness when you make your remarks. A bitter spirit is manifest in a person's tone and expression, as well as words, and makes clear to others a poor sense of self worth.

If you have checked yourself for these things, you are in good shape. Don't worry about mere factual mistakes that are easily corrected. The important thing here is not to make it worse. If someone corrects you, and you are not an expert on the subject, graciously admit you may be wrong. As the saying goes, when you find yourself in a hole, stop digging. Factual debates cannot always be settled during a conversation, but you can make a mental note to go home and do some research. Then the next time you meet, you will be in a position to correct the picture or admit it if you were wrong (gaining points for candor and humility).

Finally, in a broad sense of thinking before speaking, check the perspective and mental attitude you bring to the conversation. No one needs another curmudgeon to deal with. Cynics and fanatics drag down the level of conversation. Consider the world beautiful as well as tragic; comment on people as both noble and amusing; and reflect on yourself as imperfect yet aspiring. Aren't these better perspectives, and more valuable to add to a group conversation, than repeating stale jokes, mean-spirited gossip, or hate speech?

LIFE LESSON: Dignity

No one likes a bully, although some make us laugh when they are picking on someone *else*. The bullies we really don't like pick on us. Middle school is a breeding ground for bullies. Having taught at that level for many years, I know it well, and I wish it weren't so. Young people haven't yet built up their psychic defenses, so bullying is especially painful. But it seems to be human nature to knock others down in order to cover up our own insecurities. In order to not feel alone, we join a clique and leave others out. In order to avoid feelings of inadequacy, we point at others and pass the blame. Along the way, we all get wounded.

Donna Hicks, Ph.D., is an associate at the Weatherhead Center for International Affairs at Harvard University. She has served as an international consultant on conflict mediation in Sri Lanka, the Middle East, Colombia, and Northern Ireland. In her years of practice, Hicks discovered that, no matter what differences divide people, they all share one commonality: everybody has had his or her dignity wounded. While she was mediating a dispute between Colombian military and civilians, she was able to get both sides to admit at least to this, which initiated a careful conversation about how mutual respect might be established in the future.

Lack of respect, exclusion, and humiliation: these are some of the common occurrences to all walks of life. They speak to the universal desire to be included, listened to, and treated with dignity. Each of us deserves this kind of treatment, made as we are in the image of God, and so it hurts and makes a lasting wound when we are not treated well.

The insults of childhood and adolescence leave us tender in certain areas. Though we may appear tough and indifferent, in fact, we are quite vulnerable. When words or actions are reminiscent of wounding episodes, they awaken strong reactions. You may be unconscious of exactly why a particular action provokes such a strong reaction, but a little introspection may reveal the reason. If you have been a victim of exclusion, you are alert now to its possibility. If you have been called stupid or clumsy, you are sensitive to slights on the score of intelligence and physical grace. Some of the damage has been self-inflicted, comparing oneself to others who you think are more popular, beautiful, or accomplished. Some damage is done in love, by parents trying to challenge us to achieve. Other damage is brought on by the proverbial bully or snob. In marriage and longterm relationships, relatively minor conflicts can be exasperated by earlier, unresolved conflicts that result in "hot buttons."

Whatever the case may be, the point here is not only to treat others with respect and dignity, but also to treat yourself with care and civility. When your feelings flare up at some comment or gesture, you may be reacting to a hot button wound. Self-respect means believing oneself deserving of decent treatment. Take the time to figure out where you have been wounded, and try to come to terms with it. Make peace with your offenders, within your own mind at least, and take on new situations—and conversations—with a clean slate.

DIALOGUE: **Demanding But Fair**

Mary Lou: Think before you speak. A good idea, certainly. But we all have stories of learning this the hard way. Does anyone have one that comes to mind—and has become a funny story at last?

Peter: I once asked a woman when she was due. She said she wasn't pregnant.

Joan: Ouch.

John: In my first job after college, I worked for a very hard-driving and demanding boss. He really let me have it when I screwed up. The worst part of it was that he wasn't fair. He doled out his punishments to some of us more than others—at least it seemed that way to me. For instance, this old guy Andrew could do wrong, even though we often had to cover his butt. Anyway, one time he was letting me have it over a delayed order and I said it was Andrew's fault and explained why. That is where I should have stopped. But then I went on to complain about the boss's unfairness. He listened for a while and then raised his finger. "John," he said, "you may be right. But Andrew has been here for years—and he is not going to change or get any better. He has reached his level of competency. But you and some of the others are just starting out. I am pushing you to be better than you think you can be so that you can get farther ahead in the end. Think about that before making a judgment."

Alice: That's a good story.

John's story is an illustration of getting carried away and saying more than we intend to say. Sometimes we may think before we start speaking but forget to check ourselves along the way! It also demonstrates how sensitive we can be about unfairness and bias in others. However, John did have a valid point to raise and his boss fortunately helped clear up his sense of unfairness. Peter, on the other hand, had no excuse for the pregnancy slip.

Keep Your Cool

(And Remember Rule Two)

"I'm not funny. What I am is brave."

LUCILLE BALL
(1911-1989) Actor and comedienne

It is not easy to "keep your head when all about are losing theirs" (Rudyard Kipling)—especially if they are blaming you! But this rule—Keep Your Cool—is absolutely essential to the art of conversation. As soon as emotions rise in response to a charged subject or a cutting remark, the conversation is in danger of becoming an argument. And, as another British writer and wit once said, "The thing I hate about an argument is that it always interrupts a discussion" (G. K. Chesterton). Wit is a wonderful way to lower the temperature. But in order to wield it, you will need to keep your own wits about you.

If someone is spouting off and you are starting to smolder, take a mental step back. Ask yourself a couple of questions: why is what this person is saying making me mad? Such self-reflection works wonders when you realize that the reason we often lose our tempers over seemingly innocuous remarks is that we have certain "buttons" and sensitivities,

What pushes your buttons?

as mentioned in the previous Life Lesson, that come from hurtful episodes in our past. Sometimes our buttons are pushed by words, jokes, or points of view, but other times it is something about the person saying them, something that reminds us of someone totally different. We may feel deep resentments, often unconscious, over old violations of our dignity that are triggered in a present interaction. So a bit of reflection may help you realize you are overreacting, and your own "old baggage" is weighing you down.

Sometimes you are justifiably angry because the person irritating you is simply a jerk. Before jumping in with an emotional response, ask this question: what is the best way to deal with this person? Think tactically instead of reacting viscerally. Indeed, the secret to keeping your cool is to *act*, not *react*. The difference, as I am using the words, is that a *reaction* is dictated by the terms and tone of the original actor. But an *action* is determined by you—it's your free choice. When you act instead of react, you open the field of possible responses: you may reply with a counter-argument (keeping anger out of your voice); you may reply with a cool stare and icy body language, signal enough that the person has transgressed; or you may, as I believe is the best course of action, reply with wit and gracefully move on to a less charged subject.

The point is that you are not losing your cool even when there is an obvious slight. This signals to others that the expectations of this group include courteous manners and enjoyment of each other's company, not scoring points or changing minds.

Above all, remember what conversation is all about. It

is a means of giving each other the pleasure of company, of sharing in an exchange of rapid thought, clear ideas, and fresh expression.

Even if much of conversation does not live up to this exalted level, we can at least give it the old college try. Listen with attention—you will give pleasure to the speaker and you may even learn something. Speak with care—infrequent use of "I" and awareness of one's own internal emotional state will become habitual with practice. Cultivate wit—read widely, memorize some great quotes and stories, and keep a graceful eye on the mood of the group. Invite the quiet—be mindful of who hasn't spoken and who looked as if there was something he or she wanted to say when another person jumped in. Quiet the over-participator—the best way is to thank Jack for his contribution and praise his knowledge and insight, but say that you would also like to hear from Jill, who looked as if she had something to add a moment ago. Seeing yourself in the role of a conversational facilitator—and we all have a share—is actually a very helpful tool for keeping your cool (even when you could just kick that idiot).

LIFE LESSON: Joy

"Surely the condition of life is joy." This observation, courtesy of Henry David Thoreau, is at odds with much of our daily experience. Conflict and toil are a part of the condition of life…yet isn't it possible for joy to be present even in their midst? We do not want to concede that sadness, boredom, or anger are more fundamental; after all, these are the result of things gone wrong, such as losses, lack of fulfilling work, or injustice. No, we were made for joy: our senses and mind alive and alert, friends and loved ones beside us, a challenge facing us, and hope for a promising future. Can't you feel the wind in your face even now?

The trick is sticking with joy when things aren't so rosy, when we are tired or sick, lonely and worried. It is akin to keeping your cool when all around are losing theirs. In tough times you need to reach down and hold on to your better self. Exercise your imagination. What times in your life answered best to the description of a joyful life? Remember your feelings then? This is not just an exercise in nostalgia. For the question is whether you can look around with eyes reminded of what life can hold. Remember the joy of pure play? When you were a child the simplest things were full of wonder. Your imagination could make worlds out of cardboard, castles out of sand, forts out of pillows. When you were young and in love, the world seemed welcoming and the future full of possibility. I am old enough to have loved and lost and many youthful dreams have remained unrealized. But still I believe and try to act as if the world is made new every day. Every day something surprises me, some beauty or kindness touches me, and I can rejoice. I still love to play. And, needless to say, I love a good conversation.

DIALOGUE: Balcony View

Mary Lou: We've come to the last of the rules, and it's one of the hardest to follow. Does anyone have a story about keeping cool when the conversation got hot?

Joan: I'm scanning my memory in three categories: discussing household chores with my husband and children (where I generally lose my cool), discussing politics with Fred my idiot co-worker (conversation moves quickly to mutual exasperated disdain), or trying to talk with service personnel (being put on hold does bad things to my ability to stay calm).

Alice: Once at a dinner party, two people started getting into a heated political argument. Probably because I wasn't directly involved, I managed to stay in an observer's frame of mind. Just as the insult point was reached, I jumped in and recommended to the table that we hold an immediate election. All in favor of changing the subject raise their hands. The ayes had it, so we moved to a less charged topic.

Mary Lou: Well done, Alice.

Alice's story is a great example of keeping cool and using wit. But, as we all know, this is the hardest of all the rules when the subject or tone touches a tender spot. The thing to do is to "know yourself," as the old saying goes, and know when you need to step off the dance floor and onto the balcony for some fresh air and perhaps a new perspective. This helps a good deal—to become an observer instead of a combatant.

PART TWO

Applications

Colloquies are intentional gatherings for the purpose of entertaining conversation. Serious subjects may be broached, but the purpose is not information (we are not attending a lecture), or argument (a debate), but mutual enjoyment.

Starting a Colloquy

Now that you know the rules, it is time to get started. But of course you already have. You have been conversing since you learned to speak. Talking is part of being human, and the art of conversation is an ancient art. Socrates was a great master, and Cicero wrote a version of the rules. But the trick is mastering it. For that, you need an occasion to practice and a coach to help. You have your dinner table and family, a circle of friends who meet occasionally, and your colleagues at work or school, but do you have a place you can go where the intention is to indulge in pleasant, amusing, and informed conversation? You be the judge.

If no occasion presents itself, then perhaps it is time to drum something up. That, at least, is what I thought when I grew bored with the same loop of subjects and trivial conversation. I embarked on the task of researching the subject of conversation and began my experiment in hosting colloquies.

WHAT IS A COLLOQUY?

A colloquy (from the Latin *colloquium,* speaking together or conference) is simply "a talking together, conversation, dialogue" (Oxford English Dictionary). It is similar to the word *salon* (French for room or apartment), which brings to mind elegant gatherings filled with sparkling conversation and hosted by Parisian women of fashion. We may not attain such high society elegance, but the colloquies I organize are *intentional gatherings for the purpose of entertaining conversation.* Serious subjects may be broached, but the purpose is not information (we are not attending a lecture), or argument (a debate), but mutual enjoyment. We gather so that we may share with each other what is of interest to ourselves, and hear from others in turn. If there is wit and play, well, we are reminded of what Mr. Bennett said in Jane Austen's *Pride and Prejudice,* "What do we live for but to make sport of others and be made sport of in turn?"

Yet, although we have fun and seek amusement, the ultimate object of a colloquy is serious, to improve our ability to *converse,* the original meaning of which is to live in, as well as to talk with, the world. As Cardinal Newman said, "You cannot fence without an antagonist, nor challenge all comers in disputation before you have supported a thesis; and in like manner, you cannot learn to converse till you have the world to converse with; you cannot unlearn your natural bashfulness, or awkwardness, or stiffness, or other besetting deformity, till you serve your time in a school of manners." (John Henry Newman, *The Idea of a University,* 1853).

MY FIRST COLLOQUY

Inspired by models of past salons and symposiums, I looked around for a similar opportunity, or for a book that not only taught the history of the art of conversation, but the how to. I'm afraid I grew frustrated in both searches. There were book clubs, continuing education courses, and other opportunities for "lifelong learning." I have yet to find a book on the how to of a proper conversation (hence this effort).

Where could I practice conversation? If nowhere else, then my living room. For starters, I began to invite a few friends over, and together we teased out a format. What eventually worked was an introductory session in which we laid out some ground rules and began. As we explored different topics, we found that either a single person needed to facilitate or everyone needed to agree that all should participate and no one dominate. We also realized that our tendency in conversation was to run away with subjects, to over-use the "I" word, and other traps I have identified in this book.

We had fun—so much so that the group wanted to keep going. But I had an itch to practice with strangers, to stretch my comfort zone. Once a teacher, always a teacher. My friend Judy Goldstein introduced me to Joan Kuhn, the program director of Chappaqua Library, Chappaqua, New York. There, over a six-week period, we held the first Colloquy sessions. I did a similar set of colloquies at the public library of Fairfield, Connecticut, where Karen Roland directs programs. Both venues proved perfect. My daughter-in-law, Mary Calkins, developed some clever posters and fliers and advertised the colloquies. The idea caught on. This book is the culmination of many drafts and focus groups— some filmed—and the work of many hands and minds.

STARTING A COLLOQUY GROUP: THE NUTS, BOLTS, AND COFFEE-MAKERS

The best place to start is right at home. Invite some friends over for a colloquy; that is, a guided conversation. Send out a written invitation to make it more formal and intentional than a simple social gathering. When asked what you have in mind, explain that you are intrigued by the idea of having a wide-ranging conversation on a variety of topics—nothing set in stone, no book to read beforehand. Mention that you have learned a few tips for facilitating the conversation and would like to try them out with friends.

Keep it simple. Don't throw a three-course meal; simply provide coffee, tea, water, a few nibbles at most. You want to keep the focus on the conversation, not the food. Refrain from serving alcohol. A cocktail party moves on a different level of light and increasingly muddled small talk. If you do offer wine, drink moderately; the host's example will set the model for expected behavior.

Starting a colloquy group should also have the virtue of extending one's circle of acquaintances. The whole point is to break from stale and repetitive conversations. To accomplish this, you may want to seek neutral ground, such as a public library. Libraries are wonderful resources for communities and are often under-utilized. Many offer comfortable rooms for conversation and, by definition, they are neutral and safe public spaces. Libraries also have excellent communications resources and can help get the word out—though you will have to be proactive in designing fliers and notices. Librarians, I have found, are very interesting and helpful people—and indeed I hope they find this book and initiate a few colloquies themselves.

Another venue is an adult education program. Community colleges, senior centers, and other organizations, such as the YMCA, offer various courses on language, travel, computer skills, and so on. Why not call the coordinator of the program and offer to lead a conversation group? Keep this book at hand to bolster your confidence. You can do it!

Don't neglect emerging forms of connection through the internet. Some of these lead to actual sit-down, face-to-face conversation groups. Some have their own set of rules, too. Check out the "Brown Bag" colloquy group from Sydney, Australia, the "Conversation Cafes" begun by Vicki Robison in Seattle, and the "Socratic Cafes" organized by Christopher Philip in cooperation with Columbia University.

TOPICS, PITFALLS, AND FACILITATOR TIPS

Here is something I would like to stress: don't be afraid to talk about anything. Let the group dynamic govern what is acceptable and what, if anything, is off limits. But do be attentive to the feelings of everyone in the group. Certain topics are sure to be controversial (see next page: politics, sex, religion), so it may be best to wait until the group has learned to converse with grace, wit, and attentive listening before discussing potentially charged topics.

Topics we have covered include such standards as travel, culture (art, music, movies), and the issues and social mores of the day, compared and contrasted with those of our youth or of other epochs in history. It is fun to try and imagine the future as well. Be mindful of the tendency of age to make one nostalgic and overly eager to begin sentences with the phrase,

"When I was young." Try to include people of various ages in the group—they are sure to have different perspectives. Resist the temptation to focus on negative changes; keep balanced in emotional mood as well as participation. The facilitator will have a key role in monitoring these balances. Keeping the conversation flowing, everyone participating, and the mood enjoyable requires vigilance and a deft touch. Especially if things get heated...

WHEN THINGS GET HEATED

If talk turns to politics, sex, or religion, that is perfectly fine. Nobody wants to confine the conversation to safe and boring topics. People have differing views on politics; let them state them with care and civility. People harbor deep convictions about God and matters of ultimate concern, such as the meaning of life, the existence of God, and the role of faith and religion. This is the deep end of the pool and if the group is swimming there then you have truly entered a sacred zone of conversation. If people are comfortable talking about sex—and not just being disapproving prudes or silly adolescents—this is also a sign that the group has jelled and begun to feel that the colloquy is a safe place to get real issues on the table.

But when things get heated, as they are apt to do if someone's feathers have been ruffled or controversial topics crop up, the first thing to do is to stay cool yourself. As a facilitator it is your role to stay a bit on the outside of the fray and keep one eye on the emotional temperature of the group. It is not necessary to rush in and change the subject, unless you come to this exception: if someone has offered an insult or an especially insensitive comment, it is best to intervene immediately. A quick reminder about the tone of the comment and a call to remain respectful should do the job. Try to get in before the offended party fires back in kind! Again, wit is a wonderful tool here.

If the conversation becomes a debate, then it is also time to intervene. As the facilitator you have a certain authority; this is the time to use it. Simply state that the point of your group is conversation, not debate, and suggest it is time to move to a different topic or to allow other speakers their turns. The line between vigorous conversation and debate is a fine one and will vary with the group's dynamic. What easily happens, but must be avoided, is that two people begin going back and forth, becoming increasingly agitated, with the rest of the group watching. Experience helps, and the more you practice facilitating conversation, the better your judgment and skills will get.

If the conversation becomes a debate then it is time to change the subject. As the facilitator you have a certain authority; this is the time to use it.

When one enters the working and social interaction world, it will not be one's ability to debate but to converse that becomes important.

Table Talk

Thus far, I have been writing about conversation groups composed of adults, but conversation is for all ages, and teaching the art to young people is one of the ways we equip them for the wide and diverse world they will live in.

For many years, I taught social studies at the high school level. Social Studies is a subject that naturally encourages students to learn history, become engaged citizens, and practice articulating beliefs and questioning assumptions. Around my dining room table, I insisted that my three sons do more than grunt and answer "nothing" when questioned about what happened that day. One of the ways to draw young people out is to be specific. Instead of asking general questions about their day or what they did in school, ask about specific classes, events, and people. Offer an opening statement about a subject they know something about and ask their opinion. If you are alert to their world and genuinely interested, they will sense this and open up. For instance, remark about a new video game or sport personality that you know they are passionate about. Keep in mind that attention spans increase with maturity. Choose your moments, and refrain from using dessert as a weapon!

As children become young adults and enter college,

first jobs, and serious relationships, the length and breadth of their conversation becomes greater—sometimes the talk will go on all night! But the ability to listen, to facilitate participation of others, and to keep one's cool and use wit are not automatically acquired. The academy—a term descended from Plato's first "Academy" in which he passed on the art of Socratic questioning and philosophic inquiry— is a wonderful place for learning and debate. As we have noted, conversation is not debate—yet if there is any age when the two are practically one, it is the idealistic stage of young adulthood. So, young people, fire away with friends in the dorm or at the pub. But try also to participate in more controlled exchanges in which your listening, as well as debating, skills are honed.

Active listening not only demonstrates good manners, it also shows a refreshing lack of self-absorption, a willingness to learn, and an attractive humility. Humility, though quiet, has tremendous power. Pay attention to who receives respectful attention; often it is someone who waits for the right moment to speak and does not insist that his or her viewpoint is right. In a debate the goal is to win, but not here. What people who insist on always being right fail to realize is that others don't enjoy being wrong! And if your comments are often met with silence, I need to inform you that deafening silence is not quiet applause; it is well-mannered booing. Good ideas, clearly and sometimes even forcefully put, are always welcome, but please don't presume you have all the answers. The goal is fluid discussion: you don't want fireworks, nor do you want to kill the conversation.

The ability to converse, rather than debate, becomes

even more important for young professionals. Most work is done in teams with peers, superiors, and, soon enough, people who report to you. "Social intelligence" will begin to be rewarded more than math and verbal skills, unless one is in technical fields. The best place to increase one's social "IQ" is in conversation. Start a group. Practice the rules. You will find swimming in the wider world much easier if you have mastered the art of conversation.

Sales and marketing professionals have long known the importance of the arts of listening and persuasion. There is a wide bookshelf on the topic of "How to Win Friends and Influence People," to cite one of the classics. Indeed this book is one of the best for learning about how to listen well. But group and team dynamics are important for people in all areas of business. Improving your skill in facilitating conversation will help you immensely. Hone your thoughts into crisply delivered sentences without excessive hemming and verbal tics, and you will improve the impression you make in presentations or interviews. Having a group where you can practice these skills makes a lot of sense, so find one or start one.

If you are part of a large or mid-size company, put up a flier or other notice and see what happens. It may be as convenient as a lunchtime gathering. If you are in a small company or are self-employed, use the public library or local coffee shop as a venue. Your time will not only be well spent, but enjoyable and rewarding.

Teaching the Art of Conversation

In addition to forming colloquy groups, schools may be interested in adding a course in the art of conversation. After all, research has shown how important the skills of active listening and articulate speech are in developing social intelligence (see Howard Gardner, Daniel Goleman, and other researchers).

I have put together a preliminary curriculum. It draws heavily from, and complies with, the English Arts Core Curriculum adopted by the New York State Board of Regents in 1996. Naturally it may be adapted in any number of ways for particular ages and interests.

CURRICULUM

Introduction: The "Art of Conversation" curriculum is very flexible; it currently provides a level of specificity to existing curriculums for elementary through secondary levels. This curriculum also creates an opportunity to expand the level of specificity for colleges and businesses. It is designed to provide assistance, additions and supplements to materials already used by participators.

Philosophy: "NY State Education Department staff and educators across the state collaborated in the development, review and subsequent revisions of the core curriculum which is based on shared beliefs." Continually repeated throughout the curriculum is the desire to achieve regular opportunities to read, write, listen and speak. Competency in these skills is the shared responsibility of teachers. It is they who must must help their students learn to speak with understanding and respect for others.

Standards to Abide By: (1) To be able to have a discussion by active listening and collecting data, facts, and ideas. (2) To present a variety of perspectives, opinions and judgments on experiences, ideas, information, and issues. (3) To be able to speak/discuss for critical analysis and evaluation. (4) To show skill in social interaction, such as soliciting others' opinions and using humor to defuse tension.

Key Ideas: To achieve the ability to converse in an intelligent, enjoyable way, beginning in elementary grades, continuing through high school and into adulthood. In conclusion, if the "rules" presented in this book are mastered, participants will be able to initiate, facilitate, and benefit from stimulating discussions with a variety of people where thought-provoking topics and questions are successfully integrated.

If you are interested in creating lesson plans based on Mary Lou's Rules, you may contact Mary Calkins at marycalkins@mac.com. Guidelines for age appropriate curriculums are currently being developed.

Speak Easy Business Conversation

BY SKIP MORSE

No one can contest the time-honored proverb that states, "Build the relationship and the business will follow." Yet how many times have professional sales executives from Fortune 500 companies, as well as small to medium size businesses, unsuccessfully attempted to close a big order or business deal with key decision-makers they haven't really taken the time to know? The answer: more than you can count. If you've been in the work force for long, you've probably encountered the classic procurement executive who breathes fire and delights in watching all who approach him cower in fear. I recall one such individual who used to purchase fiberglass wire and cable insulation in high volume from one of my former companies. He would call me three times a week bellowing into the phone about lack of competitive pricing and minuscule quality problems. However, after taking him out to lunch once a month and demonstrating genuine interest in learning more about him as a person, devoted husband, and father, we became trusted friends and my business with him tripled. More importantly, his complaints stopped coming.

If more sales or business development training courses

adopted *Mary Lou's Rules for Engaging Conversation,* deal closure and sales goal achievement would gain a higher probability of success. Let's assume you want to approach a targeted prospect or enhance an existing business relationship with a customer or client. Does your approach follow the common style of aggressive dialogue that runs, "Thanks for your time today. This is why I'm here and these are my product features and benefits"? The rules of conversation showcased in this book offer a far superior approach. They seem so basic, but sales people and business executives often struggle with relationship building because their egos get in the way. If they just took a deep breath in a face-to-face meeting (or on Skype or another new millennium form of meeting) and thought about some of Mary Lou's Rules, their conversations might be a bit more productive. Let's see how.

First, by **Avoiding "I" Statements** you will demonstrate to your prospect or client that you are not the most superior human being in their lives. Instead, by backing off and asking **Probing Not Prying** questions about him or her, you will begin to obtain valuable and genuine insights that facilitate the building of sincere and trusting relationships. For example, don't march into a prospect's office and lead off by saying, "**I** really enjoyed watching that World Cup soccer match yesterday between Paraguay and Spain. **I** couldn't believe the deciding point caromed off both sides of the goal posts before going in." A far better approach would be to enter the office, take a quick look around to catch a glimpse of a photograph featuring a sleek looking sailboat with someone at the helm. This allows you to lead with, "That's a really great photo. That looks like you at the helm. Are you an avid racer?" This is a good **probing** question to break the ice and encourage further relationship-building dialogue around a subject you know the prospect is interested in. It also doesn't pry into more intimate territory had you asked, "How do you pay for such an expensive sport?"

One of the biggest obstacles to building productive one-on-one business relationships today is the lack of good listening skills. Too often customers share their opinions or valuable input with managers who are too busy thinking about what they are going to say next to **Listen** carefully. I am reminded of a recent conversation I had with a vice president of advertising from a Fortune 500 beverage company. He was frustrated because his ad agency's creative team failed to listen to his up-front research findings in order to determine how best to promote a new carbonated diet soft drink to consumers. The agency creatives had already made up their minds, ignoring the consumer research insights, and proceeded to develop TV commercials that were way off-target. In the advertising business, or any business for that matter, listening to others is critical. Don't be afraid to listen to and absorb what others have to offer. Even if you end up relying on your own expertise or creativity in a business decision, let others know you have heard them and have taken their opinions and findings into account. You have nothing to lose and possibly a great deal to gain.

Similarly, another rule of Mary Lou's that is invaluable in business is to **Learn.** Senior corporate executives tell me that many of their suppliers fail to spend sufficient time learning about their customers' products, markets, competitors, and overall business nuances to offer breakthrough, proactive solutions. This is especially important in cases where U.S companies are marketing and selling their wares and services into global markets. Golf clubs sell well in Japan, but not in Italy. Understanding local country cultures, customs and consumer behaviors is a learning experience that pays big dividends when determining how best to design, price and position your brands to maximize consumer consideration and purchase.

In today's tough economic environment, third party suppliers who know their customers' businesses inside and out have the competitive edge when it comes to getting the next lucrative assignment or contract renewal.

Lastly, in business, everyone has respect for the person who can think well under pressure and **Keep Their Cool,** whether at work or on the golf course. This admirable character trait requires us to stop and take a brief mental pause and "count to ten" as often as necessary. There is no quicker way to lose credibility, respect, and preference in the eyes of your customers, clients, employees and peers than to lose your temper. I know of one senior marketing executive who lost a major piece of business when he broke his nine iron over his knee after lofting his ball into a sand trap. His partner in that particular member-guest tournament happened to be the president of his second largest client.

In conclusion, whether you are sitting at a dinner table or in a boardroom, how you listen and what you say is vitally important. And learning the art of conversation by applying Mary Lou's Rules will serve you well whether you conduct business in Indianapolis or Istanbul.

MURRAY H. (SKIP) MORSE, JR. is owner and president of Morse Marketing Intl., LLC. His firm provides strategic marketing, advertising, public relations, and media management advisory services to many of the largest multi-national companies headquartered in America and Europe. Skip is also active in many public and private sector leadership endeavors related to health, education, culture, and the environment. He is a featured author and lecturer on topics of marketing, sales, and business communications.

ACKNOWLEDGEMENTS

This book is a collaborative effort. From the beginning, I have relied on good friends who share my interest in wide-ranging and fun conversations. The most useful exercise was inviting friends over for a series of intentional conversations. I called them colloquies. People loved the opportunity to hone their conversation skills. I particularly want to thank Jim and Joan Brown and Judy Kauffman Goldstein.

For my research on the history of the art of conversation, I relied on Stephen Miller, *A History of a Declining Art* (Yale University Press, 2006).

The investigation and colloquies continued in the public libraries of Chappaqua, New York, and Fairfield, Connecticut. I am greatly indebted to the librarians there, Joan Kuhn in Chappaqua and Karen Ronald in Fairfield. Currently I am leading a course in the art of conversation at the Collegium of Westchester Community College, and wish to thank Lorain Levy and Edith Litt for their invitation and assistance.

My son and daughter-in-law Matthew and Mary Calkins suggested we turn the colloquy idea into a book and a larger teaching project. Matt took my notes and conversations and put them into the words you have before you, and contributed much of the material contained in the "life lessons." Mary helped create marketing materials and brought in Skip Morse to help with business applications and marketing. Mary has been a driving force behind this project. We want to thank Gail Perry Johnston of Cupola Press for her creativity and guidance. My other son, Tom Calkins, has contributed his legal advice and general good common sense.

Together my three sons, their wives, my six grandchildren, and many friends have taught me far more than I can ever express. For one thing, they have always felt willing and able to jump into the conversation!

ABOUT THE AUTHORS

MARY LOU WALKER was born and raised in Los Angeles, California, but has lived and taught most of her life in Westchester County, New York. She was married to Richard Calkins, and raised three sons, Thomas, Matthew, and Anthony. She taught Social Studies in the public middle and high schools of Elmsford, New York, receiving an award in 1985 from the School of Education, State University of New York as a New York State "Teacher of the Year." Following retirement, Mary Lou began worked as a docent at Kykuit, the seasonal residence of the Rockefeller family in Tarrytown, New York. In 2005, at the age of 78 and still looking for more to do, she created the first Colloquy Course at the public library of Chappaqua, New York, expanding the program to Fairfield, Connecticut in 2007, and to Westchester Community College in 2008. She collaborated with her son Matthew to write this book and hopes to focus on teaching teachers the art of conversation.

MATTHEW CALKINS is the second son of Mary Lou Walker. His wife Mary teaches art in the Fairfield, Connecticut public school system. Matthew serves as Rector of St. Timothy's Episcopal Church in Fairfield and is working upon completion of a Doctor of Ministry degree from Hartford Seminary in Hartford, Connecticut.

www.cupolapress.com

Breinigsville, PA USA
14 September 2010
245255BV00001B/2/P